LIONS AND TIGERS
and other big cats

Written and illustrated by John Leigh-Pemberton

Happytime Books

Dutton-Elsevier Publishing Company, Inc.

New York

Cats

Cats of every kind are alike
in many ways.

Lions, tigers and the other cats
in this book are all 'cousins'
of our pet cats.

Lions

Lions live in hot places.

Once they lived in
much colder parts of the world.

Perhaps that is why the male lion
has a mane.

The female lion is called a lioness.
She does not have a mane.

Lions — where they live

Nearly all the lions in the world
live in Africa.

There are a few left in India.

Once there were a great many
there.

In Africa, lions live
on the huge, grassy plains.

They do not live in deserts,
or among mountains,
or in thickly wooded places.

Lions — how they live

Lions are hunters.

They kill and eat other animals.

When they are not hunting
they sleep for much of the time.

A pride of lions

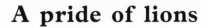

Lions live in groups.

A fully-grown male lion
rules over several lionesses,
cubs and young lions.

This group is called a pride.

Lion cubs

Baby lions are called cubs.

From two to five are born
at the same time.

Their eyes are closed at birth.

They are quite helpless.

Lion cubs, like this month-old one,
are born with spotted fur.

Cubs open their eyes after a week.
After three weeks they can walk.
As they grow up,
they lose their spotted coats.

Cubs romp and play
for much of the time.
This helps to train them as hunters.

Lions — roaring

The area lived in by a pride of lions is called a territory.

The male lion usually roars to protect his pride and territory.

Only the 'big cats' roar.

These are the lion, tiger, leopard, snow leopard and jaguar.

Lions — teeth and tongue

Like all the cat family, lions use
their large teeth to tear their food.

They do not chew their food.

They swallow it in large lumps.

Their rough tongues help them
to swallow, and to clean
and smooth down their fur.

How long do lions live?

Lions are grown-up at about four years old.

Only a few live longer than ten years.

Old lions live alone.

Lionesses usually stay with the pride all their lives.

The tiger might easily die out
as a wild animal.

If the tiger is to be saved,
men must stop hunting it.
We must not use its fur.
It must be allowed natural living
space.

Leopards — where they live

Leopards live in many kinds of country, where there are trees.

They live in jungles, forests, grassy plains and among mountains.

There are leopards in India, China and many other parts of Asia.

They are found also in most of Africa and sometimes in Persia and Israel.

Leopards' spots

Leopards are hard to see
in the leafy places where they live.

Their spotted fur looks like
a pattern of leaves and shadows.

Black leopards

Panther is another name for a
leopard.

Some Indian leopards
which are nearly black,
are often called panthers.

Their dark spots can be seen
in sunlight.

Clouded leopards

These small leopards live in the trees of thick jungles in Asia.

The pattern of their fur is hard to see among the trees.

Snow leopards

Snow leopards live among rocks
in the high, cold mountains of Asia.

Their long, pale-colored fur
is hard to see against the rocks.

Lynxes

Lynxes live in the cold parts
of America and Europe.

Their long fur keeps them warm.

Hares and birds are the main food
of lynxes and caracals.

Sometimes they kill larger animals.

Pumas

Pumas are found in many parts of North and South America.

Other names for the puma are – cougar, mountain lion, painter and catamount.

Pumas can live in all kinds of country.

Some live in deserts or mountains.

Others live in grassland or thick jungle.

Jaguars

The 'big cats' of South America
are the jaguars.

These powerful animals
live mostly in thick woodland.

The jaguar's pattern of spots
is different from the leopard's.

The jaguar has a dot in some rings
of his spots.

The leopard has no dot.

Ocelots

The ocelot is a smaller cat
of South America.

This animal has been much
hunted for its beautiful fur.

Because it has been hunted so
much, it is now becoming quite
rare.

So are many other spotted cats.

Wild cats

Wild cats live in several parts
of Europe.

Some live in Scotland.

Wild cats look very like tame cats.

They are about the same size.

Wild cats have longer legs,
thicker tails and bigger teeth.

Lions in zoos

Zoo lions usually live longer
than wild ones.

They eat about ten pounds (4.5 kg)
of meat a day.

It is natural for a lion to hunt.
Zoo lions miss being able to hunt.

Tigers — where they live

Most of the wild tigers in the world live in the jungles of India.

A few live in China and in other parts of Asia.

Tiger cubs

Three or four tiger cubs
are born at a time.
This is called a litter of cubs.

Tigers are fully grown at three
years.
They can live for twenty years.
Usually they do not reach this age.

White tigers

In one part of India
there are some beautiful white
tigers.

They have chocolate-colored
stripes and blue eyes.